My Book Journal

"A must for every reader"

BOOK CLUB

BOOKS I'VE READ & BOOKS I WANT TO READ

Books With Soul®

For Sharon Hoffman who encourages and
motivates her team to read books every
month.
Special thanks to all the readers and the
book clubs active and thriving out there in
the world. Thank you for reading books,
discussing books and loving books.

Books With Soul®
Somewhere in the desert, sea and forest.
bookswithsoul.com
∞
Books With Soul supports copyright for all authors.
Thank you for purchasing a copyrighted edition of this book.
First Edition 2019

We lose ourselves in books.
We find ourselves there too.
–Anonymous

Let's Get Lost!

Reading gives us someplace to go
when we have to stay where we are.
–Mason Cooley

Table of Contents:
Section I: Book Club Summary
One page summary for Book Club Discussions.
Fantastic Future Reference Guide.

Section II: Notes & Memories from Books Read, Book Club Meetings and Book Events.
Space for notes and journaling and rating of books.

Section III: List of Books I Read.
Space to keep lists of all the titles you
have read, date and a rating system.
Great Guide.

Section IV: Log of Books I Want to Read.
Keep a list of the top 50 books you want
to read someday.
Additional pages for a list of recommended books.
A handy list when you are looking for your next book.

"I love books it's about time I had a book to keep track of my books."
Amazon customer

"The person who deserves the
most pity is a lonesome one
on a rainy day who doesn't
know how to read."
-Benjamin Franklin

Section I
Book Club Summary
One page summary
for your next
book club.
(Fantastic Future Reference Guide)

Book Club Summary

TITLE:

DATE READ:

RATING:

★ ★ ★ ★ ★

AUTHOR

GENRE

LENGTH

CHARACTERS

KEY POINTS

Notes

Book Club Summary

TITLE:

AUTHOR

DATE READ:

RATING:

★ ★ ★ ★ ★

GENRE

LENGTH

CHARACTERS

KEY POINTS

Notes

Book Club Summary

TITLE:

DATE READ:

RATING:

★ ★ ★ ★ ★

AUTHOR

GENRE

LENGTH

CHARACTERS

KEY POINTS

Notes

Book Club Summary

TITLE:

DATE READ:

RATING:

★ ★ ★ ★ ★

GENRE

LENGTH

AUTHOR

CHARACTERS

KEY POINTS

Notes

Book Club Summary

TITLE:

DATE READ:

AUTHOR

RATING:

★ ★ ★ ★ ★

GENRE

LENGTH

CHARACTERS

KEY POINTS

Notes

Book Club Summary

TITLE:

DATE READ:

RATING:

★ ★ ★ ★ ★

AUTHOR

GENRE

LENGTH

CHARACTERS

KEY POINTS

Notes

Book Club Summary

TITLE:

AUTHOR

DATE READ:

RATING:

★ ★ ★ ★ ★

GENRE

LENGTH

CHARACTERS

KEY POINTS

Notes

Book Club Summary

TITLE:

DATE READ:

AUTHOR

RATING:

★ ★ ★ ★ ★

GENRE

LENGTH

CHARACTERS

KEY POINTS

Notes

Book Club Summary

TITLE:

DATE READ:

RATING:

★ ★ ★ ★ ★

GENRE

AUTHOR

LENGTH

CHARACTERS

KEY POINTS

Notes

Book Club Summary

TITLE:

AUTHOR

DATE READ:

RATING:

★ ★ ★ ★ ★

GENRE

LENGTH

CHARACTERS

KEY POINTS

Notes

Book Club Summary

TITLE:

DATE READ:

AUTHOR

RATING:

★ ★ ★ ★ ★

GENRE

LENGTH

CHARACTERS

KEY POINTS

Notes

Book Club Summary

TITLE:

DATE READ:

RATING:

★ ★ ★ ★ ★

GENRE

AUTHOR

LENGTH

CHARACTERS

KEY POINTS

Notes

Book Club Summary

TITLE:

DATE READ:

RATING:

★ ★ ★ ★ ★

GENRE

AUTHOR

LENGTH

CHARACTERS

KEY POINTS

Notes

Book Club Summary

TITLE:

AUTHOR

DATE READ:

RATING:

★ ★ ★ ★ ★

GENRE

LENGTH

CHARACTERS

KEY POINTS

Notes

Book Club Summary

TITLE:

DATE READ:

RATING:

★ ★ ★ ★ ★

GENRE

AUTHOR

LENGTH

CHARACTERS

KEY POINTS

Notes

Book Club Summary

TITLE:

DATE READ:

RATING:

★ ★ ★ ★ ★

AUTHOR

GENRE

LENGTH

CHARACTERS

KEY POINTS

Notes

Book Club Summary

TITLE:

DATE READ:

RATING:

★ ★ ★ ★ ★

AUTHOR

GENRE

LENGTH

CHARACTERS

KEY POINTS

Notes

Book Club Summary

TITLE:

DATE READ:

RATING:

★ ★ ★ ★ ★

GENRE

LENGTH

AUTHOR

CHARACTERS

KEY POINTS

Notes

Book Club Summary

TITLE:

DATE READ:

RATING:

★ ★ ★ ★ ★

AUTHOR

GENRE

LENGTH

CHARACTERS

KEY POINTS

Notes

Book Club Summary

TITLE:

DATE READ:

AUTHOR

RATING:

★ ★ ★ ★ ★

GENRE

LENGTH

CHARACTERS

KEY POINTS

Notes

Book Club Summary

TITLE:

DATE READ:

RATING:

★ ★ ★ ★ ★

GENRE

AUTHOR

LENGTH

CHARACTERS

KEY POINTS

Notes

Book Club Summary

TITLE:

DATE READ:

RATING:

★ ★ ★ ★ ★

GENRE

AUTHOR

LENGTH

CHARACTERS

KEY POINTS

Notes

Book Club Summary

TITLE:

DATE READ:

RATING:

★ ★ ★ ★ ★

GENRE

LENGTH

AUTHOR

CHARACTERS

KEY POINTS

Notes

Section II
Notes and Memories from book club, books read and book events.

**WHO I DISCUSSED THIS BOOK
WITH:**

DATE:

WHERE WE MET:

OTHER THOUGHTS ABOUT THE BOOK, THIS DAY, THE AUTHOR, THE CHARACTERS, MY BOOK CLUB GROUP AND EVERYTHING ELSE THAT IS GOING ON IN THE WORLD RIGHT NOW:

BOOK TITLE:

AUTHOR:

DATE STARTED READING

Give a brief summary about the book.

Fiction: who are the main characters? Non-fiction who is writing the book?

Would you recommend this book?

One phrase, idea or character I want to remember about this book:

NOTES:
What I want to remember about this moment, this book, this meeting, this year, and the message of the book.

_____

_____

_____

_____

_____

_____

_____

_____

_____

_____

_____

_____

NOTES

WHO I DISCUSSED THIS BOOK WITH: DATE:

WHERE WE MET:

OTHER THOUGHTS ABOUT THE BOOK, THIS DAY, THE AUTHOR, THE CHARACTERS, MY BOOK CLUB GROUP AND EVERYTHING ELSE THAT IS GOING ON IN THE WORLD RIGHT NOW:

BOOK TITLE:

AUTHOR:

DATE STARTED READING

Give a brief summary about the book.

Fiction: who are the main characters? Non-fiction who is writing the book?

Would you recommend this book?

One phrase, idea or character I want to remember about this book:

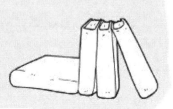

NOTES:
What I want to remember about this moment, this book, this meeting, this year, and the message of the book.

_____

_____

_____

_____

_____

_____

_____

_____

_____

_____

_____

NOTES

WHO I DISCUSSED THIS BOOK WITH:

DATE:

WHERE WE MET:

OTHER THOUGHTS ABOUT THE BOOK, THIS DAY, THE AUTHOR, THE CHARACTERS, MY BOOK CLUB GROUP AND EVERYTHING ELSE THAT IS GOING ON IN THE WORLD RIGHT NOW:

BOOK TITLE:

AUTHOR:

DATE STARTED READING

Give a brief summary about the book.

Fiction: who are the main characters? Non-fiction who is writing the book?

Would you recommend this book?

One phrase, idea or character I want to remember about this book:

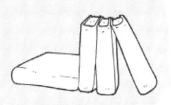

NOTES:
What I want to remember about this moment, this book, this meeting, this year, and the message of the book.

_____

_____

_____

_____

_____

_____

_____

_____

_____

_____

_____

_____

NOTES

WHO I DISCUSSED THIS BOOK WITH: DATE:

WHERE WE MET:

OTHER THOUGHTS ABOUT THE BOOK, THIS DAY, THE AUTHOR, THE CHARACTERS, MY BOOK CLUB GROUP AND EVERYTHING ELSE THAT IS GOING ON IN THE WORLD RIGHT NOW:

BOOK TITLE:

AUTHOR:

DATE STARTED READING

Give a brief summary about the book.

Fiction: who are the main characters? Non-fiction who is writing the book?

Would you recommend this book?

One phrase, idea or character I want to remember about this book:

NOTES:
What I want to remember about this moment, this book, this meeting, this year, and the message of the book.

_____

_____

_____

_____

_____

_____

_____

_____

_____

_____

_____

NOTES

**WHO I DISCUSSED THIS BOOK
WITH:**   **DATE:**

WHERE WE MET:

**OTHER THOUGHTS ABOUT THE BOOK, THIS DAY, THE AUTHOR,
THE CHARACTERS, MY BOOK CLUB GROUP AND EVERYTHING
ELSE THAT IS GOING ON IN THE WORLD RIGHT NOW:**

BOOK TITLE:

AUTHOR:

DATE STARTED READING

Give a brief summary about the book.

Fiction: who are the main characters? Non-fiction who is writing the book?

Would you recommend this book?

One phrase, idea or character I want to remember about this book:

NOTES:
What I want to remember about this moment, this book, this meeting, this year, and the message of the book.

_____

_____

_____

_____

_____

_____

_____

_____

_____

_____

_____

_____

NOTES

**WHO I DISCUSSED THIS BOOK
WITH:**

DATE:

WHERE WE MET:

**OTHER THOUGHTS ABOUT THE BOOK, THIS DAY, THE AUTHOR,
THE CHARACTERS, MY BOOK CLUB GROUP AND EVERYTHING
ELSE THAT IS GOING ON IN THE WORLD RIGHT NOW:**

BOOK TITLE:

AUTHOR:

Give a brief summary about the book.

Fiction: who are the main characters? Non-fiction who is writing the book?

DATE STARTED READING

Would you recommend this book?

One phrase, idea or character I want to remember about this book:

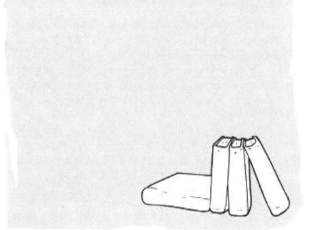

NOTES:
What I want to remember about this moment, this book, this meeting, this year, and the message of the book.

_____

_____

_____

_____

_____

_____

_____

_____

_____

_____

_____

_____

NOTES

WHO I DISCUSSED THIS BOOK WITH:

DATE:

WHERE WE MET:

OTHER THOUGHTS ABOUT THE BOOK, THIS DAY, THE AUTHOR, THE CHARACTERS, MY BOOK CLUB GROUP AND EVERYTHING ELSE THAT IS GOING ON IN THE WORLD RIGHT NOW:

BOOK TITLE:

AUTHOR:

DATE STARTED READING

Give a brief summary about the book.

Fiction: who are the main characters? Non-fiction who is writing the book?

Would you recommend this book?

One phrase, idea or character I want to remember about this book:

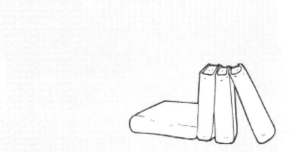

NOTES:
What I want to remember about this moment, this book, this meeting, this year, and the message of the book.

_____

_____

_____

_____

_____

_____

_____

_____

_____

_____

_____

_____

_____

NOTES

WHO I DISCUSSED THIS BOOK WITH: DATE:

WHERE WE MET:

OTHER THOUGHTS ABOUT THE BOOK, THIS DAY, THE AUTHOR, THE CHARACTERS, MY BOOK CLUB GROUP AND EVERYTHING ELSE THAT IS GOING ON IN THE WORLD RIGHT NOW:

BOOK TITLE:

AUTHOR:

DATE STARTED READING

Give a brief summary about the book.

Fiction: who are the main characters? Non-fiction who is writing the book?

Would you recommend this book?

One phrase, idea or character I want to remember about this book:

NOTES:
What I want to remember about this moment, this book, this meeting, this year, and the message of the book.

NOTES

WHO I DISCUSSED THIS BOOK WITH:

DATE:

WHERE WE MET:

OTHER THOUGHTS ABOUT THE BOOK, THIS DAY, THE AUTHOR, THE CHARACTERS, MY BOOK CLUB GROUP AND EVERYTHING ELSE THAT IS GOING ON IN THE WORLD RIGHT NOW:

BOOK TITLE:

AUTHOR:

Give a brief summary about the book.

Fiction: who are the main characters? Non-fiction who is writing the book?

Would you recommend this book?

One phrase, idea or character I want to remember about this book:

DATE STARTED READING

NOTES:
What I want to remember about this moment, this book, this meeting, this year, and the message of the book.

_____

_____

_____

_____

_____

_____

_____

_____

_____

_____

_____

_____

_____

NOTES

WHO I DISCUSSED THIS BOOK WITH: DATE:

WHERE WE MET:

OTHER THOUGHTS ABOUT THE BOOK, THIS DAY, THE AUTHOR, THE CHARACTERS, MY BOOK CLUB GROUP AND EVERYTHING ELSE THAT IS GOING ON IN THE WORLD RIGHT NOW:

BOOK TITLE:

DATE STARTED READING

AUTHOR:

Give a brief summary about the book.

Fiction: who are the main characters? Non-fiction who is writing the book?

Would you recommend this book?

One phrase, idea or character I want to remember about this book:

NOTES:
What I want to remember about this moment, this book, this meeting, this year, and the message of the book.

_____

_____

_____

_____

_____

_____

_____

_____

_____

_____

_____

_____

NOTES

**WHO I DISCUSSED THIS BOOK
WITH:**

DATE:

WHERE WE MET:

**OTHER THOUGHTS ABOUT THE BOOK, THIS DAY, THE AUTHOR,
THE CHARACTERS, MY BOOK CLUB GROUP AND EVERYTHING
ELSE THAT IS GOING ON IN THE WORLD RIGHT NOW:**

BOOK TITLE:

DATE STARTED READING

AUTHOR:

Give a brief summary about the book.

Fiction: who are the main characters? Non-fiction who is writing the book?

Would you recommend this book?

One phrase, idea or character I want to remember about this book:

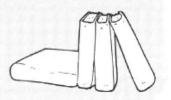

NOTES:

What I want to remember about this moment, this book, this meeting, this year, and the message of the book.

_____

_____

_____

_____

_____

_____

_____

_____

_____

_____

_____

_____

NOTES

WHO I DISCUSSED THIS BOOK WITH:

DATE:

WHERE WE MET:

OTHER THOUGHTS ABOUT THE BOOK, THIS DAY, THE AUTHOR, THE CHARACTERS, MY BOOK CLUB GROUP AND EVERYTHING ELSE THAT IS GOING ON IN THE WORLD RIGHT NOW:

BOOK TITLE:

AUTHOR:

DATE STARTED READING

Give a brief summary about the book.

Fiction: who are the main characters? Non-fiction who is writing the book?

Would you recommend this book?

One phrase, idea or character I want to remember about this book:

NOTES:
What I want to remember about this moment, this book, this meeting, this year, and the message of the book.

_____

_____

_____

_____

_____

_____

_____

_____

_____

_____

_____

_____

NOTES

WHO I DISCUSSED THIS BOOK WITH:

DATE:

WHERE WE MET:

OTHER THOUGHTS ABOUT THE BOOK, THIS DAY, THE AUTHOR, THE CHARACTERS, MY BOOK CLUB GROUP AND EVERYTHING ELSE THAT IS GOING ON IN THE WORLD RIGHT NOW:

BOOK TITLE:

AUTHOR:

DATE STARTED READING

Give a brief summary about the book.

Fiction: who are the main characters? Non-fiction who is writing the book?

Would you recommend this book?

One phrase, idea or character I want to remember about this book:

NOTES:
What I want to remember about this moment, this book, this meeting, this year, and the message of the book.

_____

_____

_____

_____

_____

_____

_____

_____

_____

_____

_____

_____

NOTES

WHO I DISCUSSED THIS BOOK WITH:

DATE:

WHERE WE MET:

OTHER THOUGHTS ABOUT THE BOOK, THIS DAY, THE AUTHOR, THE CHARACTERS, MY BOOK CLUB GROUP AND EVERYTHING ELSE THAT IS GOING ON IN THE WORLD RIGHT NOW:

BOOK TITLE:

AUTHOR:

DATE STARTED READING

Give a brief summary about the book.

Fiction: who are the main characters? Non-fiction who is writing the book?

Would you recommend this book?

One phrase, idea or character I want to remember about this book:

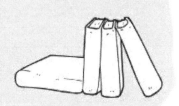

NOTES:
What I want to remember about this moment, this book, this meeting, this year, and the message of the book.

_____

_____

_____

_____

_____

_____

_____

_____

_____

_____

_____

_____

NOTES

WHO I DISCUSSED THIS BOOK WITH:

DATE:

WHERE WE MET:

OTHER THOUGHTS ABOUT THE BOOK, THIS DAY, THE AUTHOR, THE CHARACTERS, MY BOOK CLUB GROUP AND EVERYTHING ELSE THAT IS GOING ON IN THE WORLD RIGHT NOW:

BOOK TITLE:

AUTHOR:

DATE STARTED READING

Give a brief summary about the book.

Fiction: who are the main characters? Non-fiction who is writing the book?

Would you recommend this book?

One phrase, idea or character I want to remember about this book:

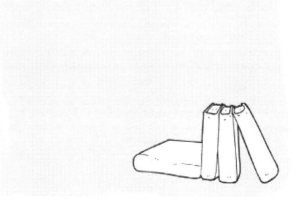

NOTES:
What I want to remember about this moment, this book, this meeting, this year, and the message of the book.

NOTES

WHO I DISCUSSED THIS BOOK WITH:

DATE:

WHERE WE MET:

OTHER THOUGHTS ABOUT THE BOOK, THIS DAY, THE AUTHOR, THE CHARACTERS, MY BOOK CLUB GROUP AND EVERYTHING ELSE THAT IS GOING ON IN THE WORLD RIGHT NOW:

BOOK TITLE:

AUTHOR:

DATE STARTED READING

Give a brief summary about the book.

Fiction: who are the main characters? Non-fiction who is writing the book?

Would you recommend this book?

One phrase, idea or character I want to remember about this book:

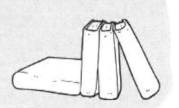

NOTES:
What I want to remember about this moment, this book, this meeting, this year, and the message of the book.

NOTES

WHO I DISCUSSED THIS BOOK WITH:

DATE:

WHERE WE MET:

OTHER THOUGHTS ABOUT THE BOOK, THIS DAY, THE AUTHOR, THE CHARACTERS, MY BOOK CLUB GROUP AND EVERYTHING ELSE THAT IS GOING ON IN THE WORLD RIGHT NOW:

BOOK TITLE:

AUTHOR:

DATE STARTED READING

Give a brief summary about the book.

Fiction: who are the main characters? Non-fiction who is writing the book?

Would you recommend this book?

One phrase, idea or character I want to remember about this book:

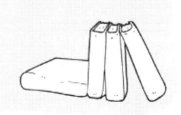

NOTES:
What I want to remember about this moment, this book, this meeting, this year, and the message of the book.

_____

_____

_____

_____

_____

_____

_____

_____

_____

_____

_____

_____

NOTES

WHO I DISCUSSED THIS BOOK WITH: **DATE:**

WHERE WE MET:

OTHER THOUGHTS ABOUT THE BOOK, THIS DAY, THE AUTHOR, THE CHARACTERS, MY BOOK CLUB GROUP AND EVERYTHING ELSE THAT IS GOING ON IN THE WORLD RIGHT NOW:

BOOK TITLE:

AUTHOR:

DATE STARTED READING

Give a brief summary about the book.

Fiction: who are the main characters? Non-fiction who is writing the book?

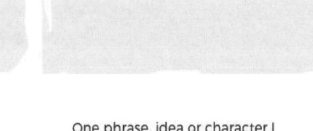

Would you recommend this book?

One phrase, idea or character I want to remember about this book:

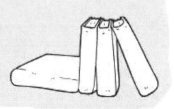

NOTES:
What I want to remember about this moment, this book, this meeting, this year, and the message of the book.

_____

_____

_____

_____

_____

_____

_____

_____

_____

_____

_____

_____

NOTES

WHO I DISCUSSED THIS BOOK WITH: **DATE:**

WHERE WE MET:

OTHER THOUGHTS ABOUT THE BOOK, THIS DAY, THE AUTHOR, THE CHARACTERS, MY BOOK CLUB GROUP AND EVERYTHING ELSE THAT IS GOING ON IN THE WORLD RIGHT NOW:

BOOK TITLE:

AUTHOR:

DATE STARTED READING

Give a brief summary about the book.

Fiction: who are the main characters? Non-fiction who is writing the book?

Would you recommend this book?

One phrase, idea or character I want to remember about this book:

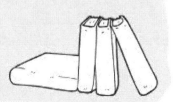

NOTES:
What I want to remember about this moment, this book, this meeting, this year, and the message of the book.

NOTES

**WHO I DISCUSSED THIS BOOK
WITH:**

DATE:

WHERE WE MET:

**OTHER THOUGHTS ABOUT THE BOOK, THIS DAY, THE AUTHOR,
THE CHARACTERS, MY BOOK CLUB GROUP AND EVERYTHING
ELSE THAT IS GOING ON IN THE WORLD RIGHT NOW:**

BOOK TITLE:

AUTHOR:

DATE STARTED READING

Give a brief summary about the book.

Fiction: who are the main characters? Non-fiction who is writing the book?

Would you recommend this book?

One phrase, idea or character I want to remember about this book:

NOTES:

What I want to remember about this moment, this book, this meeting, this year, and the message of the book.

_____

_____

_____

_____

_____

_____

_____

_____

_____

_____

_____

_____

_____

_____

NOTES

WHO I DISCUSSED THIS BOOK WITH:

DATE:

WHERE WE MET:

OTHER THOUGHTS ABOUT THE BOOK, THIS DAY, THE AUTHOR, THE CHARACTERS, MY BOOK CLUB GROUP AND EVERYTHING ELSE THAT IS GOING ON IN THE WORLD RIGHT NOW:

BOOK TITLE:

AUTHOR:

DATE STARTED READING

Give a brief summary about the book.

Fiction: who are the main characters? Non-fiction who is writing the book?

Would you recommend this book?

One phrase, idea or character I want to remember about this book:

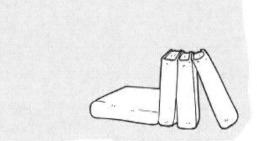

NOTES:
What I want to remember about this moment, this book, this meeting, this year, and the message of the book.

_____

_____

_____

_____

_____

_____

_____

_____

_____

_____

_____

_____

_____

NOTES

**WHO I DISCUSSED THIS BOOK
WITH:**

DATE:

WHERE WE MET:

**OTHER THOUGHTS ABOUT THE BOOK, THIS DAY, THE AUTHOR,
THE CHARACTERS, MY BOOK CLUB GROUP AND EVERYTHING
ELSE THAT IS GOING ON IN THE WORLD RIGHT NOW:**

BOOK TITLE:

AUTHOR:

DATE STARTED READING

Give a brief summary about the book.

Fiction: who are the main characters? Non-fiction who is writing the book?

Would you recommend this book?

One phrase, idea or character I want to remember about this book:

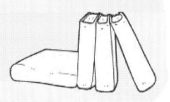

NOTES:
What I want to remember about this moment, this book, this meeting, this year, and the message of the book.

_____

_____

_____

_____

_____

_____

_____

_____

_____

_____

_____

_____

_____

NOTES

WHO I DISCUSSED THIS BOOK WITH:

DATE:

WHERE WE MET:

OTHER THOUGHTS ABOUT THE BOOK, THIS DAY, THE AUTHOR, THE CHARACTERS, MY BOOK CLUB GROUP AND EVERYTHING ELSE THAT IS GOING ON IN THE WORLD RIGHT NOW:

BOOK TITLE:

AUTHOR:

DATE STARTED READING

Give a brief summary about the book.

Fiction: who are the main characters? Non-fiction who is writing the book?

Would you recommend this book?

One phrase, idea or character I want to remember about this book:

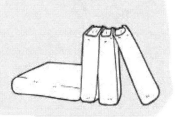

NOTES:
What I want to remember about this moment, this book, this meeting, this year, and the message of the book.

_____

_____

_____

_____

_____

_____

_____

_____

_____

_____

_____

_____

_____

_____

NOTES

NOTES

"I guess there are never
enough books."
-John Steinbeck

Section III
LOG OF THE BOOKS
I'VE READ

So many books so little time...

If you want to rate each book, use 1-5 with 1 being the lowest and 5 being an outstanding read.

Books Read

Year _

Books

TITLE/AUTHOR/YEAR	DATE READ:	RATING
		★ ★ ★ ★ ★
		★ ★ ★ ★ ★
		★ ★ ★ ★ ★
		★ ★ ★ ★ ★
		★ ★ ★ ★ ★
		★ ★ ★ ★ ★
		★ ★ ★ ★ ★
		★ ★ ★ ★ ★
		★ ★ ★ ★ ★
		★ ★ ★ ★ ★
		★ ★ ★ ★ ★
		★ ★ ★ ★ ★
		★ ★ ★ ★ ★
		★ ★ ★ ★ ★
		★ ★ ★ ★ ★
		★ ★ ★ ★ ★
		★ ★ ★ ★ ★
		★ ★ ★ ★ ★
		★ ★ ★ ★ ★
		★ ★ ★ ★ ★

FAVORITE READS OF THE YEAR	AUTHOR	EBOOK OR PRINT	RATING

Books Read

Year __

Books

TITLE/AUTHOR/YEAR	DATE READ:	RATING
		★ ★ ★ ★ ★
		★ ★ ★ ★ ★
		★ ★ ★ ★ ★
		★ ★ ★ ★ ★
		★ ★ ★ ★ ★
		★ ★ ★ ★ ★
		★ ★ ★ ★ ★
		★ ★ ★ ★ ★
		★ ★ ★ ★ ★
		★ ★ ★ ★ ★
		★ ★ ★ ★ ★
		★ ★ ★ ★ ★
		★ ★ ★ ★ ★
		★ ★ ★ ★ ★
		★ ★ ★ ★ ★
		★ ★ ★ ★ ★
		★ ★ ★ ★ ★
		★ ★ ★ ★ ★
		★ ★ ★ ★ ★

FAVORITE READS OF THE YEAR	AUTHOR	EBOOK OR PRINT	RATING

Books Read

Year _

Books		
TITLE/AUTHOR/YEAR	**DATE READ:**	**RATING**
		★ ★ ★ ★ ★
		★ ★ ★ ★ ★
		★ ★ ★ ★ ★
		★ ★ ★ ★ ★
		★ ★ ★ ★ ★
		★ ★ ★ ★ ★
		★ ★ ★ ★ ★
		★ ★ ★ ★ ★
		★ ★ ★ ★ ★
		★ ★ ★ ★ ★
		★ ★ ★ ★ ★
		★ ★ ★ ★ ★
		★ ★ ★ ★ ★
		★ ★ ★ ★ ★
		★ ★ ★ ★ ★
		★ ★ ★ ★ ★
		★ ★ ★ ★ ★
		★ ★ ★ ★ ★
		★ ★ ★ ★ ★
		★ ★ ★ ★ ★

FAVORITE READS OF THE YEAR	AUTHOR	EBOOK OR PRINT	RATING

Books Read

Year _

Books

TITLE/AUTHOR/YEAR	DATE READ:	RATING
		★ ★ ★ ★ ★
		★ ★ ★ ★ ★
		★ ★ ★ ★ ★
		★ ★ ★ ★ ★
		★ ★ ★ ★ ★
		★ ★ ★ ★ ★
		★ ★ ★ ★ ★
		★ ★ ★ ★ ★
		★ ★ ★ ★ ★
		★ ★ ★ ★ ★
		★ ★ ★ ★ ★
		★ ★ ★ ★ ★
		★ ★ ★ ★ ★
		★ ★ ★ ★ ★
		★ ★ ★ ★ ★
		★ ★ ★ ★ ★
		★ ★ ★ ★ ★
		★ ★ ★ ★ ★
		★ ★ ★ ★ ★

FAVORITE READS OF THE YEAR	AUTHOR	EBOOK OR PRINT	RATING

Books Read

Year _

Books		
TITLE/AUTHOR/YEAR	DATE READ:	RATING
		★ ★ ★ ★ ★
		★ ★ ★ ★ ★
		★ ★ ★ ★ ★
		★ ★ ★ ★ ★
		★ ★ ★ ★ ★
		★ ★ ★ ★ ★
		★ ★ ★ ★ ★
		★ ★ ★ ★ ★
		★ ★ ★ ★ ★
		★ ★ ★ ★ ★
		★ ★ ★ ★ ★
		★ ★ ★ ★ ★
		★ ★ ★ ★ ★
		★ ★ ★ ★ ★
		★ ★ ★ ★ ★
		★ ★ ★ ★ ★
		★ ★ ★ ★ ★
		★ ★ ★ ★ ★
		★ ★ ★ ★ ★
		★ ★ ★ ★ ★

FAVORITE READS OF THE YEAR	AUTHOR	EBOOK OR PRINT	RATING

Books Read

Year _

TITLE/AUTHOR/YEAR	DATE READ:	RATING
		★ ★ ★ ★ ★
		★ ★ ★ ★ ★
		★ ★ ★ ★ ★
		★ ★ ★ ★ ★
		★ ★ ★ ★ ★
		★ ★ ★ ★ ★
		★ ★ ★ ★ ★
		★ ★ ★ ★ ★
		★ ★ ★ ★ ★
		★ ★ ★ ★ ★
		★ ★ ★ ★ ★
		★ ★ ★ ★ ★
		★ ★ ★ ★ ★
		★ ★ ★ ★ ★
		★ ★ ★ ★ ★
		★ ★ ★ ★ ★
		★ ★ ★ ★ ★
		★ ★ ★ ★ ★
		★ ★ ★ ★ ★

FAVORITE READS OF THE YEAR	AUTHOR	EBOOK OR PRINT	RATING

Books Read

Year _

Books

TITLE/AUTHOR/YEAR	DATE READ:	RATING
		★ ★ ★ ★ ★
		★ ★ ★ ★ ★
		★ ★ ★ ★ ★
		★ ★ ★ ★ ★
		★ ★ ★ ★ ★
		★ ★ ★ ★ ★
		★ ★ ★ ★ ★
		★ ★ ★ ★ ★
		★ ★ ★ ★ ★
		★ ★ ★ ★ ★
		★ ★ ★ ★ ★
		★ ★ ★ ★ ★
		★ ★ ★ ★ ★
		★ ★ ★ ★ ★
		★ ★ ★ ★ ★
		★ ★ ★ ★ ★
		★ ★ ★ ★ ★
		★ ★ ★ ★ ★
		★ ★ ★ ★ ★
		★ ★ ★ ★ ★

FAVORITE READS OF THE YEAR	AUTHOR	EBOOK OR PRINT	RATING

Books Read

Year ___

	Books	
TITLE/AUTHOR/YEAR	**DATE READ:**	**RATING**
		★ ★ ★ ★ ★
		★ ★ ★ ★ ★
		★ ★ ★ ★ ★
		★ ★ ★ ★ ★
		★ ★ ★ ★ ★
		★ ★ ★ ★ ★
		★ ★ ★ ★ ★
		★ ★ ★ ★ ★
		★ ★ ★ ★ ★
		★ ★ ★ ★ ★
		★ ★ ★ ★ ★
		★ ★ ★ ★ ★
		★ ★ ★ ★ ★
		★ ★ ★ ★ ★
		★ ★ ★ ★ ★
		★ ★ ★ ★ ★
		★ ★ ★ ★ ★
		★ ★ ★ ★ ★
		★ ★ ★ ★ ★

FAVORITE READS OF THE YEAR	AUTHOR	EBOOK OR PRINT	RATING

Books Read

Year _

Books

TITLE/AUTHOR/YEAR	DATE READ:	RATING
		★ ★ ★ ★ ★
		★ ★ ★ ★ ★
		★ ★ ★ ★ ★
		★ ★ ★ ★ ★
		★ ★ ★ ★ ★
		★ ★ ★ ★ ★
		★ ★ ★ ★ ★
		★ ★ ★ ★ ★
		★ ★ ★ ★ ★
		★ ★ ★ ★ ★
		★ ★ ★ ★ ★
		★ ★ ★ ★ ★
		★ ★ ★ ★ ★
		★ ★ ★ ★ ★
		★ ★ ★ ★ ★
		★ ★ ★ ★ ★
		★ ★ ★ ★ ★
		★ ★ ★ ★ ★
		★ ★ ★ ★ ★
		★ ★ ★ ★ ★

FAVORITE READS OF THE YEAR	AUTHOR	EBOOK OR PRINT	RATING

Books Read

Year _____

Books

TITLE/AUTHOR/YEAR	DATE READ:	RATING
		★ ★ ★ ★ ★
		★ ★ ★ ★ ★
		★ ★ ★ ★ ★
		★ ★ ★ ★ ★
		★ ★ ★ ★ ★
		★ ★ ★ ★ ★
		★ ★ ★ ★ ★
		★ ★ ★ ★ ★
		★ ★ ★ ★ ★
		★ ★ ★ ★ ★
		★ ★ ★ ★ ★
		★ ★ ★ ★ ★
		★ ★ ★ ★ ★
		★ ★ ★ ★ ★
		★ ★ ★ ★ ★
		★ ★ ★ ★ ★
		★ ★ ★ ★ ★
		★ ★ ★ ★ ★
		★ ★ ★ ★ ★

FAVORITE READS OF THE YEAR	AUTHOR	EBOOK OR PRINT	RATING

Books Read

Year ___

	Books	
TITLE/AUTHOR/YEAR	**DATE READ:**	**RATING**
		★ ★ ★ ★ ★
		★ ★ ★ ★ ★
		★ ★ ★ ★ ★
		★ ★ ★ ★ ★
		★ ★ ★ ★ ★
		★ ★ ★ ★ ★
		★ ★ ★ ★ ★
		★ ★ ★ ★ ★
		★ ★ ★ ★ ★
		★ ★ ★ ★ ★
		★ ★ ★ ★ ★
		★ ★ ★ ★ ★
		★ ★ ★ ★ ★
		★ ★ ★ ★ ★
		★ ★ ★ ★ ★
		★ ★ ★ ★ ★
		★ ★ ★ ★ ★
		★ ★ ★ ★ ★
		★ ★ ★ ★ ★

FAVORITE READS OF THE YEAR	AUTHOR	EBOOK OR PRINT	RATING

Books Read

Year __

Books

TITLE/AUTHOR/YEAR	DATE READ:	RATING
		★ ★ ★ ★ ★
		★ ★ ★ ★ ★
		★ ★ ★ ★ ★
		★ ★ ★ ★ ★
		★ ★ ★ ★ ★
		★ ★ ★ ★ ★
		★ ★ ★ ★ ★
		★ ★ ★ ★ ★
		★ ★ ★ ★ ★
		★ ★ ★ ★ ★
		★ ★ ★ ★ ★
		★ ★ ★ ★ ★
		★ ★ ★ ★ ★
		★ ★ ★ ★ ★
		★ ★ ★ ★ ★
		★ ★ ★ ★ ★
		★ ★ ★ ★ ★
		★ ★ ★ ★ ★

FAVORITE READS OF THE YEAR	AUTHOR	EBOOK OR PRINT	RATING

Books Read

Year _

	Books	
TITLE/AUTHOR/YEAR	**DATE READ:**	**RATING**
		★ ★ ★ ★ ★
		★ ★ ★ ★ ★
		★ ★ ★ ★ ★
		★ ★ ★ ★ ★
		★ ★ ★ ★ ★
		★ ★ ★ ★ ★
		★ ★ ★ ★ ★
		★ ★ ★ ★ ★
		★ ★ ★ ★ ★
		★ ★ ★ ★ ★
		★ ★ ★ ★ ★
		★ ★ ★ ★ ★
		★ ★ ★ ★ ★
		★ ★ ★ ★ ★
		★ ★ ★ ★ ★
		★ ★ ★ ★ ★
		★ ★ ★ ★ ★
		★ ★ ★ ★ ★
		★ ★ ★ ★ ★
		★ ★ ★ ★ ★

FAVORITE READS OF THE YEAR	AUTHOR	EBOOK OR PRINT	RATING

Books Read

Year _

Books

TITLE/AUTHOR/YEAR	DATE READ:	RATING
		★ ★ ★ ★ ★
		★ ★ ★ ★ ★
		★ ★ ★ ★ ★
		★ ★ ★ ★ ★
		★ ★ ★ ★ ★
		★ ★ ★ ★ ★
		★ ★ ★ ★ ★
		★ ★ ★ ★ ★
		★ ★ ★ ★ ★
		★ ★ ★ ★ ★
		★ ★ ★ ★ ★
		★ ★ ★ ★ ★
		★ ★ ★ ★ ★
		★ ★ ★ ★ ★
		★ ★ ★ ★ ★
		★ ★ ★ ★ ★
		★ ★ ★ ★ ★
		★ ★ ★ ★ ★
		★ ★ ★ ★ ★

FAVORITE READS OF THE YEAR	AUTHOR	EBOOK OR PRINT	RATING

Books Read

Year ___

Books

TITLE/AUTHOR/YEAR	DATE READ:	RATING
		★ ★ ★ ★ ★
		★ ★ ★ ★ ★
		★ ★ ★ ★ ★
		★ ★ ★ ★ ★
		★ ★ ★ ★ ★
		★ ★ ★ ★ ★
		★ ★ ★ ★ ★
		★ ★ ★ ★ ★
		★ ★ ★ ★ ★
		★ ★ ★ ★ ★
		★ ★ ★ ★ ★
		★ ★ ★ ★ ★
		★ ★ ★ ★ ★
		★ ★ ★ ★ ★
		★ ★ ★ ★ ★
		★ ★ ★ ★ ★
		★ ★ ★ ★ ★
		★ ★ ★ ★ ★
		★ ★ ★ ★ ★

FAVORITE READS OF THE YEAR	AUTHOR	EBOOK OR PRINT	RATING

Section IV
LOG OF THE BOOKS
I WANT to READ

So many books, so little time...
A place to log the top 50 books
you would like to read.

My top List of Books I want to read:

Title: Author:

_____

_____

_____

_____

_____

_____

_____

_____

_____

_____

_____

_____

My top List of Books I want to read:

Title: Author:

_____

_____

_____

_____

_____

_____

_____

_____

_____

_____

_____

_____

_____

_____

When I need a good book, here is a list of Books I want to read :

Title: Author:

_____

_____

_____

_____

_____

_____

_____

_____

_____

_____

_____

_____

_____

When I need a good book, here is my top 15 books to read:

Title: Author:

_____

_____

_____

_____

_____

_____

_____

_____

_____

_____

_____

_____

_____

_____

My list of Books I want to read :

Title   Author:

_____

_____

_____

_____

_____

_____

_____

_____

_____

_____

_____

_____

Books with Soul ™

was inspired from a lover of music and life, who believed in the soul. He had a collection of wonderful things. Physical memories you could read, touch, and listen to-including thousands of vinyl albums.

Old school music, that lasts forever. In 2018, he passed away from brain cancer, but his memory lives on as others go old school. Collect pieces of your history, put pencil to paper, and record written memories.

A physical book will not be lost in the cloud and will last longer than a lifetime.

Keep a record of the story of your life. Your Words. Your Pages.

- This is for you Mark.

Other Books With Soul on Amazon:
Go to: amazon.com/author/bookswithsoul
Travel Junkie: The History of Me
Run Away With Me- Travel Log book
Words I want to Say
Every Breath- A Journal of Gratitude & Blessings
Pregnancy Journal: When we were one
Positivity Journal: Just Breathe
Do It Now Journal: I'd Pick More Daisies
Remember When: Guest Book
Camp Memories
Reflections from the Beach
The Plan
The Adventures of US
Reflections of My Year
Travel Log & Journal: I Was Here
Wish: A book of wishes
Dirt Road Diaries: My off-road adventures
Hunting Season logbook
My Travel Bucket List
Old Soul: a notebook of ideas

Made in the USA
San Bernardino, CA
05 August 2019